# Why Doesn't Pizza Grow on Trees?

Written by Michelle Ansani

Illustrated by Award-Winning Artist,
Rosemarie Gillen

# Why Doesn't Pizza Grow on Trees?

ISBN-13: 978-0692535981
ISBN-10: 0692535985

MLA
Labels, LLC.

For Aidan and Viv.
Keep dreaming, never stop
learning and always believe
that anything is possible.

# This Book Belongs To:

_____

My sister Suzie's best friend is Lucy.
She lives in the house at the end of
the street

and in her backyard,
is a great big orange tree.

Bobby-Joe, who I used to know
lives on a road
called Cherry Nut Rose.

He has a lemon tree, as high as a tower.
He picks them and eats them,
he likes that they're sour.

By a very small house, on the edge of the land
Kade walks his dog, in the soft white sand.

He walks and he walks,
until he gets to his tree
with big brown coconuts
and even bigger green leaves.

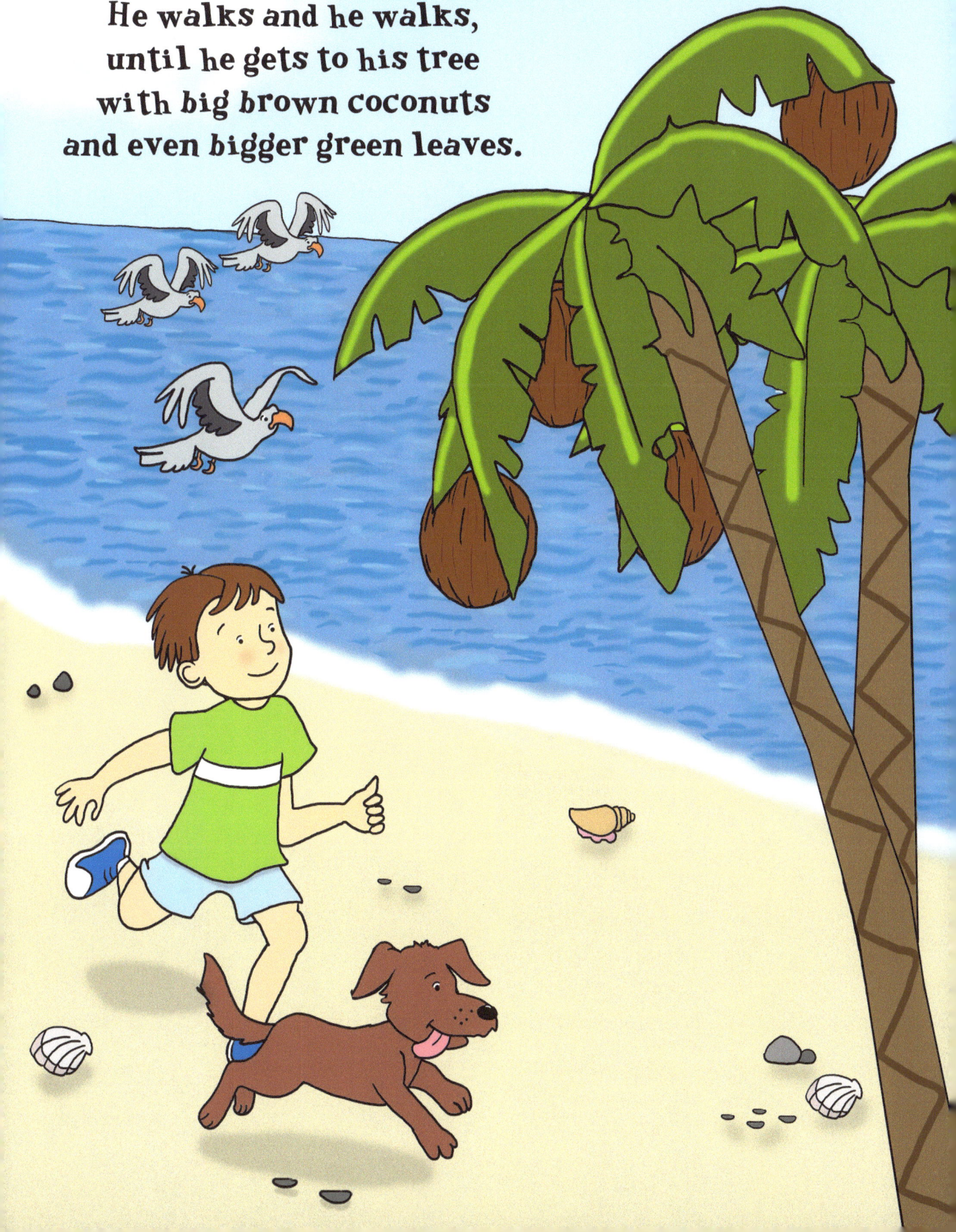

My father's best friend and his daughter Briella
moved down by the water to live in Australia.

They eat fish for their dinner and off to the side
is a big ripe banana, that's sugared and fried.

I once read a story about Jac and his uncle.
They live and they farm way deep in the jungle.

They grow great big pineapples,
under the bright Kenya sun.
I'm not sure how they do it,
but it sure sounds like fun.

I just met a girl, her name is Khadijah.
She's new to my school;
she moved from Malaysia.

If I get a chance, I'd like to go
to climb up a tree,
and pick a super sweet mango.

Ollie and Olivia are very best friends.
They laugh and they play
they jump and they climb
and when they are done

they like to eat grapes,
from their very own vine.

My friend has a friend, his nickname is Rome.
He lives in a village,
on a street made of stone.

He likes to eat figs from right off his tree.
He doesn't eat one, instead he eats three.

My name is Aidan
and I love to dream
and if I could imagine MY favorite tree

it would grow pizza
and it would grow just for ME.

Why Doesn't Pizza Grow on Trees?